# Contents

# Sarah's birthday

On her birthday Sarah had some
birthday cards, some presents
and a birthday cake with six candles.

There are six candles because
Sarah is six years old.
One candle for every year.

She likes to look at photos of herself when she was just a baby.

She thinks she is very grown up now.

# Mum's birthday

Ruth is Sarah's Mum.

On her birthday she will be thirty-five years old.

Ruth shows Sarah some more photos. Sarah likes to see photos of Ruth when she was young.

Ruth

Ruth's gran

Ruth

# Sarah's Gran

Sarah's Gran often comes to stay.

On her birthday she will be sixty-one.
She's the oldest.
She's twenty-six years older than Ruth
and fifty-five years older than Sarah.

She has some photos of herself
when she was young too.

Sarah's gran

Gorflwsfa Boarding School, 1934

Daniel has a new baby brother.
His name is Carl.

They have a Mum called Julie,
a Gran called Helen,
a Great-gran called Beatrice and
a Great-great gran called Hannah.

The five generations got together
for Carl's christening party.

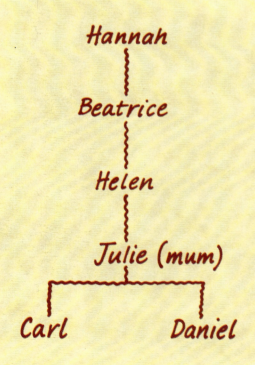

*Hannah*

*Beatrice*

*Helen*

*Julie (mum)*

*Carl*          *Daniel*

# A centenarian

Alfred is one hundred years old.

On his birthday he had one hundred candles on his cake, one for each of the years since he was born.

He also had a telegram from the Queen.

He has some photographs to show people
what he looked like as a young man.

Alfred when he was sixty.

Alfred when he was forty.

Alfred when he was twenty-four.

No one knows what Alfred
looked like when he was
a baby.
No one in his family had
a camera then.

Cholmondeley sisters c. 1600

Here is a very old painting.
It was painted four hundred years ago,
the day the babies were born.

Their mothers are sisters.

Each sister had a baby on the same day.

Look at the mothers.
Look at the babies.

Layette, Hever Castle, Kent

Four hundred years ago babies wore clothes like this.

They slept in cradles made of wood like this.

16th century cradle

Sometimes places have birthdays too.

When this school had been open for twenty-five years the children had a special party. It was called a 'Silver Jubilee Party.'
There were twenty-five candles on the birthday cake.

The Priory Infant School, Cambridge 1976

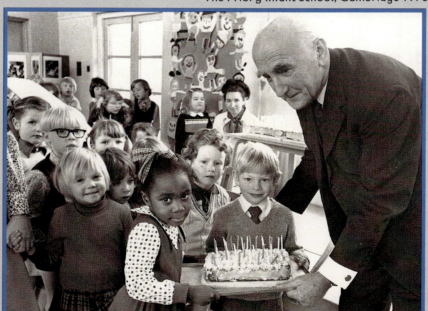

St. Philip's C of E Primary School, 1900

This school had a centenary party.
It was one hundred years old.
The teachers found some old photos.
The children looked at the photos
to find out what it was like at the school
a hundred years before.

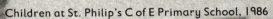
Children at St. Philip's C of E Primary School, 1986

Children at St. Philip's C of E Primary School, 1900

# A city celebration

The big city of Birmingham
had a centenary too.

There were lots of exciting
things to do.

Corporation St., Birmingham, 1990

Children at school went in for a competition.

They looked at old buildings
and new buildings.

They looked at old photographs.

They tried to find out if
Birmingham had changed.

Corporation St., Birmingham, 1897

# Anniversaries

Sometimes birthdays are called anniversaries.
An anniversary comes every year.
Some anniversaries are special.

After twenty-five years there is a
silver jubilee anniversary.

After fifty years there is a golden anniversary.

A one hundred year anniversary
is called a centenary.

Who would you give these cards to?